ONE STEP, THE FIRST STEP

Everything in Life Can Be Accomplished in Step One

I0541551

BY:

STEPHANIE WELKER

THE FIRST STEP: PUTTING YOURSELF FIRST

"Faith is taking the FIRST STEP,

even when

you don't see the whole staircase."

-   Martin Luther King, JR

THE FIRST STEP: PUTTING YOURSELF FIRST

My Story

I had a rough childhood. My father and I didn't have a relationship until I was a young adult, and my mother—an alcoholic—often had abusive boyfriends around when she wasn't off on drinking binges, regularly leaving me and my brother to fend for ourselves for days at a time. And even though we lived in low-income housing, and relied on welfare, my mother still managed to get us evicted from every place we lived turning our lives into cycles of getting kicked out, living in shelters, motel rooms, and staying with friends' families.

It felt like all my brother and I had was each other. Then, when I was 14, my brother, turning 16, he got into some trouble and was sentenced as an adult, handing him long prison term resulting in me feeling completely alone (as I am sure he did as well). By 15, I had enough of trying to carry the weight of my mother's problems: I decided to go out on my own. I moved to another state and stayed with a friend's family for a couple of months while looking for a job and saving money.

During that time, I met a woman who felt like a mother figure. She told me I could get a small studio apartment in her building if I could pay upfront with cash, no ID required. The place was a converted row home split into apartments. The neighborhood wasn't any better than the one I'd just left in Baltimore, but it gave me something I hadn't had before—total independence and freedom. And that was everything to me.

I've been on my own ever since.

I learned early on that the only person I could truly rely on was myself, and I was perfectly fine with that. Having unqualified total freedom was exhilarating. There were plenty of good times—

mostly spent getting into trouble—but I learned valuable lessons, especially during the hardest moments. Those experiences showed me exactly what I never wanted to go through again, so I knew something had to change.

It wasn't until my twenties, after a few moves across state lines and hitting rock bottom, then getting pregnant, that I finally accepted it was time to get my life together—at least enough to grow and support a little human. Years of trial and error, outside of being a new mother, left me feeling lost and uncertain, afraid of what lay ahead. But somehow, I kept pushing forward. And over time, I started to see real change.

From there, my growth and lifestyle had certainly been a roller coaster of highs and several lows: the lessons, values, and personal growth have outweighed all lows exponentially. I learned to have gratitude and love for every moment life has to offer.

Your Story

O ut of everything you could be doing right now, you're choosing to read, to learn, to seek wisdom, to grow, to want more, have more, and do more. Truly, that's something to be proud of.

The question is: What's your story? What brought you here? What's been holding you back? What do you need to move beyond where you are right now? Who do you believe you need to be in order to succeed?

As you go through this book, you'll find the clarity and direction you need to move forward with confidence and strength. But let me be clear —it won't be easy. Success demands hard choices and a firm commitment to discipline.

The Pep Talk

My goal for you, as we move through this short, but impactful journey is to share years of experience and practical, life-changing exercises in a way that feels simple and accessible. I want to help you see the world around you with new eyes—to show how much easier life can feel when you cut out the noise, take responsibility, and focus on just one thing: **The First Step.**

As you begin, start paying close attention to the conversations you have with the people in your life. This will trigger awareness of your inner-self and your perception of the world surrounding you. You may start to notice that some people no longer belong in your inner circle—or at least not so close to your personal space.

With each step in this book, as you take ownership of your choices and continue showing up for yourself, you'll learn something valuable: the right decision for you isn't always the easiest choice to make.

But,

in the end,

it always turns out to be the clearest—and the most fulfilling—choice of all.

"It is in your moments of decision that your destiny is shaped."

- **Tony Robbins**

THE FIRST STEP

Table of Contents

Section 3: Implementation Phase

THE FIRST STEP

SECTION 1

Learning Phase

Chapter 1:

No Excuses

Even as a kid, I knew I was different. My mind was always in survival mode, constantly searching for ways to become independent. How can I make money? How can I support the people around me? How can I live on my own? How can I get away from these people? How can I be the one who makes it? How can I be the first person I know to go to college, the first to earn real money, and the first to break the cycle and build generational wealth for my family? What can I do to show the world I can succeed? And more than anything—how can I prove to myself that I can succeed?

Who do I have to become to be The First?

Why me?   ...Why not me?

As much as I knew I was different, I often caught myself making excuses—sometimes with not even realizing it. I'd think things like, I don't have a proper education. I don't have anyone to help me succeed. Only people with money know how to make more money. That "poor me" mentality crept in constantly: My family doesn't come from money. I don't have any connections. I don't even have family I can truly depend on.

Other times, I'd find myself overwhelmed—not knowing how to start, where to start, or what I could possibly do. So, I'd give up and just keep working my butt off, collecting a paycheck barely big enough to get by. In my head, I'd tell myself, when something good happens, something bad always follows, so what's the point in trying? To me, asking for help meant relying on someone else—and that made me feel weak and incapable. I told myself I only needed me: I didn't need anyone else. The excuses, the negative self-talk, the self-loathing: There were so many things I told myself about why I couldn't make it.

To me, "making it" meant earning a hundred thousand dollars in a year. At the time, that felt just as impossible as making millions. I had dropped out of school in the ninth grade. I didn't even have a bank account. How in the world could I ever make over ONE HUNDRED THOUSAND DOLLARS in a single year?! I had every excuse screaming in my head. But then there was this one quiet voice in the back, softly asking,

Why not me?

That "Why not me?" voice is often the spark—the shift—that pushes you to believe you can go further than you ever thought possible. It's the whisper that dares you to dream, even when all the noises in your head are saying you can't. Even when your current circumstances show no signs of hope. That, Why Not Me is the deep knowing inside of you that keeps you moving forward.

Let's look at some of the most common excuses we tell ourselves. Check or circle the ones that resonates with you or feels familiar:

o *Not well-connected?*

o *Not educated enough?*

o *Not attractive enough?*

o *From a poor community?*

o *Not financially stable enough?*

o *Are you too young—or too old?*

o *From a single-parent household?*

o *Don't know where to start—or what to do?*

Shut down all those negative, self-doubting excuses right now. Because in reality, those thoughts are just reasons we create in our mind to justify why we can't start or succeed. But the truth is, we're afraid.

Something is holding you back. There's a fear deep inside that needs to be faced—something you need to name and admit to yourself. Until you bring that fear to the surface and deal with it, you'll keep coming up with new excuses that sound logical but aren't real.

Let's get to the heart of it so we can move forward with a clearer, stronger mindset. No pressure—we'll be revisiting this throughout our journey.

Take a moment to write down everything you honestly believe is working AGAINST you.

Be honest. Be real.

_____

_____

_____

_____

_____

_____

_____

_____

_____

_____

Now, let's take a moment to focus on a few of these. Start by rewriting the first one here:

_____

_____

Think before you respond—Is this really true about you? Will this belief hold you back in life? Is there anyone else on this planet who's faced something similar—or who might feel the same way about themselves?

A few common excuses...

Problem: I'm not smart enough.

First, ask yourself: Are you truly not smart? I'd bet the answer is no. You're likely very capable of holding your own in just about any situation— which means you at least have street smarts and solid common sense. However, if you want to "smarten" up, you can absolutely build your skills, starting with your vocabulary.

Empowering Solution: Empower yourself by picking up a vocabulary workbook. Just one or two pages a day is enough to get started.

You may not know everything right away, but over time, you'll start recognizing new words—and using them. Reading a few pages a day from varies literature will help with this as well.

<u>Problem</u>: Unhappy with your body causing low self-esteem.

First off, self-esteem shouldn't be tied to your body type. Looks don't determine success. People of all shapes and sizes have built wealth, and some of the so-called "least attractive" people out there are happily in love. But this isn't about them—it's about how you feel in your own skin.

Empowering Solution: If your body is holding back your confidence, do something about it. Hire a personal trainer. Local trainers—those looking to build their portfolios—usually offer affordable rates and meal plans. If getting in shape is what you believe will boost your happiness, then invest in it. Get someone who can hold you accountable and help you stay consistent.

Problem: Not educated enough.

First, you need to define what that actually means to you. Are you saying you're not educated enough for a leadership role? Not educated enough to feel comfortable in a boardroom full of people in suits and ties? Break down exactly what area you feel underqualified in.

And You can't say "everything," because not everything applies to who you envision yourself becoming. So, narrow your focus. Get clear on where you see yourself, and build from there. That said, there are steps you can take to shift your mindset and grow in the areas you care about most.

Empowering Solution: Take a course at your local community college.

Many continuing educational programs offer practical, self-paced options at low cost. In 2023, I took an online leadership course for under $150. It was flexible, informative, and even came with a Certificate of Completion.

In all these examples,

It's not about knowing how to do everything right away, it's about understanding that most of the excuses we tell ourselves aren't actually true. In fact, many of them are easy to overcome once we're willing to take small steps forward.

Besides, thousands of people before you have thought the same things you're thinking or have previously worried about your same concerns and, guess what, many of them went on to exceed their expectations becoming extremely successful in life—on their terms. Success doesn't look the same for everyone, but it always starts with getting honest, taking action, and knowing what you want.

The only guaranteed way to fail is through inaction—laziness, giving up, blaming others, or refusing to get started.

Decide right now: Will you let your excuses hold you back, or will you finally admit that self-doubt and self-pity are just that—excuses? Acknowledge them. Have your moment. Then move forward.

Thoughts will run through your mind all day long. It's your job to recognize which ones are helping you—and which ones are hurting you. Identify them. Call them out. Let the negative ones go, then build on the positive ones. At the end of the day, only you can make or break you.

"If you really want to do it, you do it. There are no excuses."
- **Bruce Nauman**

No Excuses: Goals/To do

Include any self-doubt or obstacles you anticipate. Rewrite everything you believe is holding you back—no filter.

_____

_____

_____

_____

_____

_____

_____

_____

_____

_____

_____

Now, how many of them are actually bullshit?

_____

_____

Chapter 2:

Reading To Learn

"Literacy is a bridge from misery to hope."
-   **Kofi Annan**

Whatever "making it" means to you, reading will help get you there. It gives you a guide—someone by your side—as you **Move in Silence**. And by silence, I mean keep your hopes and dreams protected, away from the noise of outside opinions. If the people around you aren't earning the kind of money you want to make, or they're not in the place you're aiming for, don't waste your time discussing your goals with them. They won't see your vision. They can't offer the kind of advice you need—because they've never been where you're going.

If you want real, helpful advice—read. Reading clears the path ahead by helping you avoid unnecessary struggles. You get to learn from those who've already made it. It gives you access to wisdom from some of the greatest minds in history—knowledge that spans centuries and is right there for the taking.

Sadly, the average American doesn't fully grasp just how valuable reading undoubtedly is. If they did, they wouldn't settle for average: they'd be building greatness—like you are. You are better than the average American. You're the one out of hundreds who separates yourself from the majority. The one who clears your mind of clutter and dares to escape into the world of your wildest dreams. You are the dreamer. The doer. The one who elevates others, even when your surrounding environment tries to pull you down.

Set your standards. Then move accordingly.

Reading is your superpower. It's your quiet tool. Your secret weapon. It's how you gain the knowledge to become who you're meant to be.

"Once you learn to read,

you will be forever free."

\- **Frederick Douglass**

Let's say you're ready to land your first real job. Where do you begin? You could start by visiting the website of companies of interests, review their job openings and qualifications, then learn how to adjust your resume' to reflect what they're looking for. If you need help, there are tons of books and online resources on resume' writing that can help your application stand out.

If saving money appeals to you, you might consider purchasing a book on building financial stability, preparing for retirement, or getting started with investments—stocks, maybe a side business, Certificates of Deposit (CD), or rental and other real estate property.

If you've already been saving and want to learn how to grow your savings, there are books for that, too.

There are books on just about anything you can imagine. My advice? Keep an open mind and read whatever benefits you—your health, your future, your mindset, your faith, or anything else that deepens your understanding of a particular self-improvement topic. You might even begin with the biography of someone very well off. No matter how you feel about "rich" people, remember— they're giving you the knowledge and opportunity to create wealth and prosperity for generations through the narrative of their road to success. So don't be narrow-minded, embrace a variety of genres, cultures, beliefs, and perspectives.

And don't say you can just "YouTube it." YouTube is simply a video-based form of basic learning. It's often someone sharing what they've learned through trial and error, now confident enough to teach others. But a book offers more depth—it thoroughly explores details and helps you relate to real-life scenarios through their ups and downs, and, bonus, it's a powerful tool for strengthening your brain.

As mentioned, the world's most successful, influential, and inspiring individuals have written and read books to get where they are. There's a saying: The difference between millionaires and the average person is the library they keep in their home—or lack thereof.

"A room without books is like a body without a soul."

- **Marcus Tullius Cicero**

A few of my favorite books...

Thinking of starting a business.
"Think and Grow Rich."
By Napoleon Hill

Quick reads with profound insight.
"Who Moved My Cheese?"
By Dr. Spencer Johnson

"The Richest Man In Babylon"
By George S. Clason

Speaks to your soul.
"Daring Greatly" by Brene' Brown

"Worthy" by Jamie Kern Lima

Eye-Openers.
"The Secret" by Rhonda Byrne

"The 48 Laws of Power"
By Robert Greene

There are so many incredible books, I could go on for days giving recommendations, however; It's all about what appeals to you and what your goals and inspirations are that will have books speaking to you, as they do me.

Reading: Goals/To do

What are 2 goals you currently have?

_____

_____

Two book titles pertaining to your goals?

_____

_____

_____

Two people who achieved those goals?

_____

_____

Name an inspirational speaker who you feel is most aligned with the person you're becoming?

_____

_____

_____

_____

_____

Chapter 3:

Setting Goals

Without goals what keeps you going? Who inspires you? You need a "why" to push you through those moments when you don't feel like you're enough. Even something as simple as checking off a to-do list can trigger a sense of achievement. No matter how small the task, your brain experiences a little boost that feels good.

Each positive moment motivates us to create another. The trick is finding ways to do this without feeling overwhelmed. Setting goals helps us make progress—one step at a time. It helps us to prioritize, gives us direction, and keeps us from being scattered and unproductive.

One of the greatest gifts we have as humans is the ability to control ourselves. We can't control what others say or do, but we can control how we respond. We also get to decide what matters to us, which helps us set meaningful goals.

Your goals can be as small or as ambitious as you like. You get to decide what benefits you right now, and what sets you up for the future by entertaining multi-level goals. As you should know, it's not enough to write down a goal, you must follow through to completion or decide to scratch it. There is no in-between, decisiveness sets the standard. And standards eliminate uncertainties.

Levels of Goal Setting,

Small goal: Making your bed.

I'm going to get out of bed, do a quick stretch, fix my covers, and fluff my pillow. That way, when it's time to sleep tonight, my bed will feel cozy and inviting.

Medium goal: Buying a motorcycle.

I'm going to buy the motorcycle first, then learn to ride it. I've already set a purchase date in April. Setting a date makes it real and keeps me from making excuses.

Big goal: Going to Maui. Getting my Master's Degree.

I'll book that Maui trip now and make payments if needed. Or, I'll enroll today and take the first step toward earning my master's degree.

The "how" will come later. Right now, it's irrelevant. Don't let fear of failure or unfinished goals stop you from setting new ones. You can set as many goals as you want—and you're allowed to change your mind as often as you need.

What matters most is that you keep growing, keep setting new goals, keep moving forward, and keep building your own drive and ambition.

Every single day, you have the power to choose: to do things differently, to change your mind, to try again, or to let something go and start fresh. It's your choice. Whether you're just beginning or further into your life's journey, as long as you're alive, you can still pursue your dreams instead of settling for less or remaining complacent.

Take inspiration from the woman in her eighties who became a competitive bodybuilder, if she could reshape her entire body at that age, you can absolutely set your goals—and reach them too. In the next section, jot down some goals:

- Immediate / Short-term
- 6 months to 1 year / Mid-term
- 3 to 5 years / Long-term

**"A goal properly set
is halfway reached."**

\-   **Tom Ziglar**

Setting Goals: Goals/ To do

Small Goals:

_____

_____

_____

_____

_____

Median Goals:

_____

_____

_____

_____

_____

Grand Goals:

_____

_____

_____

_____

_____

6-Month Goals:

_____

_____

_____

_____

_____

1-Year Goals:

_____

_____

_____

_____

_____

5-Year Goals:

_____

_____

_____

_____

_____

_____

Chapter 4:

Money In, Money Out

I t's time to take responsibility for your financial future. Relying on bank cards direct deposit, credit cards, or phone applications to manage your money can create a false sense of security. This often leads to growing debt, little to no savings, and living paycheck to paycheck. It can distort your perception of how much money you truly have. A credit card isn't free money: It's simply a tool—used to build and improve a score that helps you look credit-worthy enough to buy big-ticket items like a car or a home.

Furthermore, money doesn't define your worth: Who you are and how you carry yourself matters far more. Still, money can influence how you feel about yourself—and how you feel about yourself does shape your sense of self-worth.

A lot of people connect having more money with being more valuable as a person. But that's just a feeling—not a fact.

That said, being buried in unnecessary debt is overwhelming. It can lead to stress, insecurity, self-doubt, and in some cases, hopelessness. So why keep adding that kind of pressure to your life? Concocting complaints and excuses won't lead to any solutions: it is time to have an honest conversation with yourself—admit it if you're an over spender. Take ownership. Start making changes to get your finances back on track.

Begin by separating worthy debt from unjustified debt: Mortgage, education loans, and reliable transportation, that's debt with a purpose. The rest? Probably not.

To tackle your overspending habit, try one of these two methods:

1. **Cash In Hand:** Take all the money you have and lay it out in front of you in cash. Physically seeing it can be a powerful wake-up call.
2. **Pen and Paper:** Write down your income, expenses, and financial goals. This will give you a clear picture of where you are and where you need to go.

First way: Money in hand, lay it all out creating four piles,

- Investments
- Bills
- Weekly/biweekly necessities
- Play money

Investments: Monies you will use to invest in you. From day one, make it a habit to prioritize your growth and financial stability. Start with a liquid emergency fund. The amount is up to you, begin with a small percentage of your income—even if it's just 1% or five dollars.

Visualize it: Set that pile of cash money right in front of you. That is all you have.

Side note: To better understand the concept of paying yourself first, consider: The Richest Man in Babylon by George S. Clason.

Bills: List every bill you have. Figure out how many times you get paid each month and break your expenses down accordingly. This will help you allocate your income more efficiently.

Note: In the chapter on Building Your Financial Foundation, we will cover strategies to help you avoid falling into unnecessary debt.

Weekly or Biweekly Necessities: How often you get paid will determine how much to set aside for everyday essentials. We all have things we need to get through the week—groceries, household items, gas, and so on. Setting aside a consistent amount each payday helps build better habits. Some weeks, you might splurge on name-brand items or little extras. Other weeks, you may need to go generic or skip something altogether. That's okay.

Play Money: It's important to set aside a little money just for fun—whether it is creating new memories or indulging in a sweet treat. Without play money you may find yourself overspending on impulse. If you've only have $10, get creative. Maybe grab a cheap coffee on Monday or order a cheese pizza on Friday.

Whatever is left after covering your investments, bills, and necessities—that's your play money.

Again, Lay the cash out in front of you.

No backup cards. No "I'll just put it on credit and pay it off next month." No eating out. No gas station drinks. No bar nights. If all you've got is $10 to play with, that's it. Stick with it.

The Pen and Paper Method

Writing everything down is an option—but it's not as powerful as seeing your cash in front of you. This method takes more discipline. If you struggle with managing money, do NOT rely on pen and paper.

Go the extra mile—withdraw the cash then lay it out in front of you. This hands-on approach helps you face your finances head-on. Laying out the physical cash, as your only resource for spending, for 2–3 months will change the way you choose to spend money. I promise—it works.

Take your first step toward a better financial future. Otherwise, it'll get lost in a sea of excuses, procrastination, and forgetfulness.

Learn to do it NOW.

Show up for yourself NOW.

Money In/Out List

What are your absolute monthly bills?

_____

_____

_____

_____

_____

List weekly/biweekly necessities.

_____

_____

_____

_____

How much money do you bring in each pay?

_____

_____

Investment total: $ _____ or Percent _____

Bills Total: _____

Necessities total: _____

Left over play money total: _____

When your mind is wondering about the unknown, I want you to immediately ask yourself this very simple question:

Am I sick or am I healthy?

Someone reposted this on TikTok (not sure who to give credit to for the content), it's THE BEST, and needed to be shared. Story time...

In life we only EVER have 2 things to worry about,

Are you sick or are you healthy.

If you are healthy, you have nothing to worry about. If you are sick, there are 2 things you need to worry about,

Are you going to get better or get worse.

If you get better, you don't have nothing to worry about. If you get worse, you have 2 things to worry about,

Are you going to die or are you going to live.

If you live, you don't have nothing to worry about. BUT if you die, you have 2 things to worry about,

Are you going to Heaven or are you going to Hell.

If you go to heaven, you don't have nothing to worry about. If you go to hell, Well NOW, you have 2 things to worry about,

Crispy or Extra Crispy.

Section One

Recapitulation

O ur minds come equipped with a built-in "fight or flight" response system—constantly scanning for reasons why we can't do something, be something, or have something. This internal warning system fuels thoughts like, "I'm not good enough, worthy enough, talented enough, or connected enough." It backs up our fears with "logic" pulled from past experiences or learned behaviors, trying to keep us "safe."

But what feels like protection often turns into false beliefs that hold us back. By trying to avoid discomfort, that same system turns fear (fright) into avoidance (flight). Instead of facing challenging moments head-on, we make excuses. Excuses that ultimately sabotage ourselves causing us to avoid starting, or finishing what really matters—our goals.

In Chapter One, **No Excuses,** we learned how to quiet the "flight" response by recognizing the excuses we tell ourselves as false truths. We then committed to stop listening to our doubts and start trusting our hearts. Our hearts speak the real truth: We are capable, ready, and fully equipped to accomplish our goals—just as we are.

When we write down our goals and seek guidance—whether by learning how to achieve them or reading about a mentor who embodies the success we strive for—we gain the knowledge and confidence to take action.

Reading to Learn prepares our minds for the journey ahead. It shifts our mindset from "there's no way" to "this might actually be possible." As excuses dissolve, opportunities begin to emerge. That moment of connection, when we realize, "If they can do it, so can I," sparks the belief—success is within our reach. It's fascinating how our mind can work for us or against us.

In the chapter, **Money In, Money Out,** we talked about how living paycheck to paycheck often comes from the mistaken belief that we have more money than we actually do. That false sense of security can lead us even deeper into debt through spiral and careless spending.

To begin your journey toward becoming a more financially confident and capable version of you, I recommend starting with this powerful book:

The Automatic Millionaire
by David Bach

The concept of the book encourages automating your monthly payments to aid in reaching a state of wealth, rather than relying on sheer willpower.

It offers simple but effective tips for prioritizing saving money and managing your finances more responsibly. Of course, you might find other books that speak more directly to your goals depending on your current financial situation.

The chapter on **Setting Goals** helped you break your goals down into different levels than turn them into manageable, actionable steps. While setting goals can feel exciting, going after them often requires sacrifice. It is important to decide now what you're willing to give up in order to stay focused and committed, regardless of how much support, or lack thereof you get along the way.

In the Learning Phase Section: No Excuses, Reading To Learn, Money In and Money Out, and Setting Goals. These are the foundational basis for the journey that lies ahead.

In the next section, The Eliminating Phase: we take it a step further.

SECTION 2

Eliminating Phase

Chapter 5:

Environment Means Nothing

I thank my mother for showing me who I didn't want to be—because that helped me figure out who I did want to become. At times, our environment shapes us into the person we're meant to be, even if it's hard to see the value in it at the time.

We all face different challenges—physical, mental, and emotional—that could easily become excuses for why we think we're not capable. But why let them? Why give space in your mind to yet another reason telling yourself that you're not good enough to succeed? As we've learned, the mind has a way of convincing us we're not capable or good enough, it's our job to recognize those lies than consciously flip them.

The only way to develop a winning mindset and move forward in life is to shift your perspective. Can you always change your environment? Maybe not. But can you change the way you see yourself? Absolutely, you can. Give yourself some grace. Understand that where you are right now doesn't define you—and it certainly doesn't limit where you can go or who you can become.

How is your environment holding you back?

_____

_____

_____

In what ways can you change it? Could you get a better job—or take on a second job?

_____

_____

_____

_____

In what ways can you shift your thinking to see where you are might not be so bad? (Do you have a place to sleep? Food to eat? Etc.)

Name a few things about your environment you genuinely appreciate.

_____

_____

_____

_____

Remember,

Your current situation does not define who you are, nor your worth.

This is just where you are today, it is not a reflection of what your future holds. If you ever feel otherwise, listen to Steve Harvey. He has tons of YouTube videos and audiobooks you can play while commuting, going for a jog, or walking on the treadmill. You will learn that he, like many others, came from nothing and went on to build an empire. With time and effort, you will come to realize that the feeling inside—the one whispering you're meant for more, will overpower all those negative thoughts that creep in when life begins to challenge you. And that's all those periods in life are: rough moments. Frustrating, temporary moments. Moments that are meant to challenge you, then pass.

"Our days of making it through hard times is 100%"

-Attributed to Steve Harvey

Circling back to environment, illnesses, money, age, or any other factors—let's call them what they really are: Excuses. Take a few moments to acknowledge them. Start by writing down how each of these feel like they're holding you back.

Let's start with your environment.

Environment is the surroundings or conditions in which a person lives in a particular geographical area affected by human activity. Do you see how non-personal and non-emotional that statement is? Yet, people still feel this is the place they will forever be. How might your living conditions limit you?

Environmental Factors Holding You Back:

_____

_____

_____

Illnesses, a disease, or period of sickness affecting the body or mind—conditions often are subjective experiences that are not commonly backed by medical diagnosis. In simple terms, **objective** means something is based on facts and remains the same regardless of how you feel. **Subjective,** on the other hand, is shaped by your personal feelings and your interpretation. A good example of this is body dysmorphic disorder—a condition where someone's view of their appearance is distorted by their emotions rather than any neutral or factual assessment. For instance, you believe your body size is preventing you from living a better life.

Illness (Subjective) Factors Holding You Back:

_____

_____

_____

Money factors holding you back:

_____

_____

_____

Anything else you feel is holding you back?

_____

_____

_____

All your responses are between you and you. There is no judgment here. These exercises are meant to help you get a clearer understanding of where you stand, so we can figure out how to move forward.

Shifting the focus.

How Can These "Factors" Benefit You?

What strengths can you pull from your current environment—how can this shape your future?

_____

_____

_____

_____

Money: Benefitting factors come from understanding your financial situation then identify steps to make improvements—we'll dive deeper in upcoming chapters.

Illnesses: Look back at anything negative you wrote down. Ask yourself—how many of these are actually true? Are they REALLY holding you back?

_____

_____

Shifting our focus:

Write a minimum of 10 things you love or genuinely admire about yourself. It could be anything—from your beautiful eyes to your sharp mind. **Must be 10.**

_____

_____

_____

_____

_____

_____

_____

_____

_____

_____

What kind of environment do you see yourself living in someday? What type of home comes to mind? Which city or state do you love to call home? How much land would you want? What about the view—do you imagine a country setting, a cityscape, a beachfront, or a quiet mountainside retreat?

Don't hold back—Dream big.

_____

_____

_____

_____

_____

_____

_____

_____

_____

_____

_____

_____

_____

_____

_____

_____

"A man is not old until regrets take the place of dreams"

- John Barrymore

Chapter 6:

Eliminating People

Your only purpose in life is to become the best version of yourself. That alone is enough to prove you're already winning. Being true to who you are in every moment—with genuine joy and gratitude—the ultimate victory. A mindset of ongoing learning and growth will naturally lead you toward your best self.

Set goals, absolutely—but release the pressure to meet other people's expectations. The only expectations that matter are the ones you define. Learn to embrace and enjoy this ever-evolving journey, knowing that life isn't meant to be taken too seriously, this is especially true when it comes to reassessing the people in your closest circle.

Humor will become one of your greatest allies; without it, you may take things too personally and end up feeling hurt.

I challenge you to listen, with intent, when people are speaking. Notice the words they use, their body language, and how they are engaging with you.

- ✓ Do they listen when you speak, or are they just waiting for their turn to jump in and shift the conversation back to themselves?

- ✓ Do they speak with purpose, or do they just talk to hear their own voice?

- ✓ Do they offer honest reflection, or are they full of excuses and lacking accountability?

- ✓ Do they have goals and taking actionable steps towards achieving them or are they simply coasting through life?

- ✓ Are they genuinely good, humbled people who move with integrity and grace? Or are they undercover chaos causing people?

Negative cues to look for...

Eliminate these people: These individuals need to be either removed from your life or kept at a significant distance from your inner circle.

Example 1:

You: My day has been aggravating.

Them: Yeah, my day has been blah, blah, blah.

Reason: They didn't ask any questions about your statement and immediately redirected the conversation to themselves.

Example 2:

You: I'm going to the gym after work.

Them: I was going to go to the gym, but blah, blah, blah...

Reason: They're trying to appear relatable then follow with excuses showing a lack of accountability—an attempt to justify their laziness, and a subtle competitiveness—all while, once again, shifting the focus back to themselves.

Example 3:

You: I'm going back to college to get my {insert degree type}.

Them: Why? That's such a waste of time. Lots of people succeed without a degree. It costs so much money. How are you going to afford it? I wish I had the time or money, but blah, blah...

Reason: They're judgmental, unsupportive, and offering unsolicited, negative opinions. Their hidden jealousy reveals as they try to discourage you from pursuing something that matters to you.

As you begin to notice the difference between what people are actually saying and what you've been interpreting they are saying, you'll start to tune out the negative energy of those who aren't showing up for themselves—or for you—in any meaningful way. Moving forward, when intently listening during conversations, take their words at face value, do not try to find meaning behind what you think they are saying. If you're unsure— ask!

Positive cues to look for...

Keep these people: These are the individuals you want in your inner circle.

Example 1:

You: My day has been aggravating.

Them: What's been aggravating about it? Want to grab a drink later to turn things around? Is there anything I can do to help? Do you need to vent? If so, would you rather I just listen, or are you looking for advice?

Reason: Supportive, attentive, and caring. They listen with intention, offer comfort, and ask what you need so they can provide the right type of support.

Example 2:

You: I'm going to the gym after work.

Them: Need a push-you-harder partner? What are you working on today? Look at you getting in shape—that's awesome! You're inspiring me to get back into the gym. Thank you! Get it, girl! Bro, that's what's up! Leg day?

Reason: They act as your cheerleader. They're excited about your progress, asking thoughtful questions, and bring positive energy with genuine compliments and playful motivation.

Example 3:

You: I'm going back to college to get my {insert degree type}.

Them: That's amazing! I'm so happy for you. I know you've got this. Let me know if you ever need a study partner. It's going to be a long road, but I believe in you and know you'll succeed. I'm here for you through the struggles—whatever you need, I've got your back.

Reason: They're encouraging and fully invested in your growth. They recognize the effort it takes to reach your goal and are willing to walk with you, support you, and stand by you every step of the way.

Surround yourself with people who share your positive mindset—those who set goals, chase dreams, take actionable steps, stay driven, and hold themselves accountable. It's often said that you're only as strong as the weakest person in your circle.

That doesn't mean you can't have associates or acquaintances, but those relationships should remain surface-level. When engaging with them, stick to lighthearted topics—like the weather or playful banter. Keep it fun and casual, then exit the conversation gracefully. There's no need to dive into deeper, value-based discussions when you already know they'll turn negative or become about seeking validation. This rule applies to family too.

Speaking of, when it comes to family, distancing yourself might be the hardest step—especially if you feel pressured to meet their expectations or earn their approval. The key is to identify who you're seeking approval from and ask yourself why you feel the need to prove something to them.

For me, I realized I wanted to show the people around me that I could make it. Deep down, I also wanted to prove it to myself. I believed that by showing them I could succeed, I was confirming it for me too. But in truth, the need to prove something to others only reveals self-doubt.

Proving is doubting. Let go of that mindset—it serves no purpose and only holds you back.

The Elimination Process will not be easy emotionally. You are going to be faced with tough decisions, especially when it involves stepping back from people you care about. But as we've learned, the right choice isn't always the easy choice.

As you begin the elimination process, ask yourself these two questions:

1. **Are my conversations driven by real value—do they focus on,**
   - o **Goals**: Yours or theirs
   - o **Complimentary:** Not forced
   - o **Encouraging**: Honest support
   - o **Positivity:** Minimal complaining
   - o **Growth:** What you are implementing to improve yourself—or what they are doing to grow themselves.

- o **Money:** Are you learning from people who are financially ahead of you?

If **90–95%** of your conversations aren't rooted in these kinds of topics, it's time to change how you communicate—or change who you are communicating with.

Same deal, if even **30%** of your conversations revolve around the following topics, it's time to pause and seriously evaluate yourself and your inner circle. Bringing us to the 2nd question,

2. **Are my conversations driven by nonsense—Is the focal point regarding,**
   - o **Complaining:**
     - Spouting "woe is me" stories
     - Dwelling in self-doubt, negative self-talk
   - o **Making excuses:** Always a reason why you or they can't or won't do something
   - o **Anticipating the end:** Waiting for you to finish so they can take the spotlight again

- o **Negative small talk:**
  - Social media gossip
  - Their job: Coworkers
  - Spreading ugly gossip
  - Complaining about traffic

If any of these scenarios apply, you need to bow out immediately from the conversation or else you will get sucked into the nonsense. Those individuals need to reevaluate their lives or find a hobby that brings them joy. Either way, it's not your job to make them happy or keep them entertained. In most cases, they'll stay unhappy—and that's perfect, let them remain in their unhappy lane while you move on to bigger and better things. I promise you, as you grow, cutting certain people off will start to feel natural—and you won't feel that initial guilt.

When you're focused on meaningful, productive actions you will begin to understand how valuable your time really is. Loneliness gets replaced with faith, drive, and self-discovery.

You'll learn that talking without purpose is pointless—and usually reveals a good amount about someone's finances and lack of direction. Goal-oriented people are built differently, they structure their day around how much value they can create for themselves and others.

"Toxic people attach themselves like cinder blocks tied to your ankles, and then invite you for a swim in their poisoned waters."

- **John Mark Green**

Elimination:
People That Got to Go

Eliminating:

_____

_____

_____

_____

Keeping:

_____

_____

_____

Why Keeping?

_____

_____

"Be cautious with what you feed your mind and soul. Fuel yourself with positivity and let that fuel propel you into positive action."

-   **Steve Maraboli**

Chapter 7:

Keeping It on The Surface

As imperative as it is when keeping associates, acquaintances, and even some family members at surface level when it comes to details about your personal life, social media falls into the same importance—just in a slightly different way. You can share meaningful thoughts and useful recommendations without revealing too much about your true self or what is actually going on in your life.

Many people utilize these social platforms to seek, what they consider, positive attention and validation, often without realizing the opposite effect it has. Instead of posting shallow content, focus on sharing inspirational, motivational, or practical tips for building a positive mindset and lifestyle. This lets you connect with others while still keeping things at a healthy distance.

When people mostly post the highlights of their lives—like their best selfies, extravagant meals, or vague calls for attention such as, "Please pray for me"—it often creates a façade. These "living my best life" moments usually reflect an inner emptiness, a need for validation to feel worthy.

Even worse, are the ones who use social media to broadcast someone else's lowest moments, share their personal struggles, or highlight others in their most vulnerable states—such as after a car accident or during drug use. These behaviors reveal poor character by exploiting the pain and misfortune of others just to gain attention by way of likes and comments on their post.

I'm not saying you shouldn't post the occasional selfie if you need a little boost—but aim to keep 99% of your content light and surface-level. Focus on making your posts positive, educational, and informative. This is the version of yourself you choose to let the world see—or not see at all.

Think of it this way: two extremes, but both grounded in reality.

1. If the highest executive in the industry you aspire to be in were to view your profile, how would you want to come across? What impression would you want them to leave with?

2. If the worst person imaginable were to look at your profile, what details would you want to keep hidden? What parts of your life or identity would you prefer to protect?

The smartest way to use social media is to treat each platform as a chance to learn, to grow in understanding, and then pass those values on to others. For example, you could...

❖ **Gain Knowledge:** No matter your goals— short or long-term: connect with people on social media who are where you want to be. Follow them. Learn from them. Observe how they operate. Use their success as a guide.

❖ **Gain Wisdom:** Look for meaningful, and uplifting content that speaks to you. Follow pages that share motivational speeches or encouraging quotes, podcasts, or anything that pushes you to grow. Surround yourself with positive messages and people who help you become better.

❖ **Giving to Others:** Sharing inspiring and mood-lifting content. Highlight upcoming volunteer events or ways you're helping your community. Aim to become a source of encouragement. If a friend posts something that seems like a cry for attention, check in with them. Suggest a fun day out to help lighten their mood and remind them they are not alone.

The goal is to make the most of online platforms that give you access to people and knowledge you might not have otherwise. Use social media to pick up real-life lessons and find direction as you grow into the person you want to be.

Study the lives of those who inspire you. Identify the top five people in the industry you want to be part of, follow their profiles, and soak up all you can from their experiences and advice.

If you feel audacious, send a message to someone you admire: someone who's had an impact on your journey. Thank them for their influence, or recognize the challenges they've faced that made them relatable and gave you the confidence to believe that if they could succeed, so can you.

Social media can be a helpful tool for personal growth and self-improvement—if you use it with purpose and a desire to learn and grow.

"Social media is about the people! Not about your business. Provide for the people, and the people will provide for you."

- Brian Solis

"Don't use social media to impress people; use it to impact people."

- Dave Willis

Keeping It on The Surface: Goals / To Do

Your social media platforms:

_____

_____

_____

Who needs to be removed:

_____

_____

_____

Are there changes that need to be made to your post and/or images? _____

Who can you add to bring inspiration?

_____

_____

Who can you add that is currently where you want to be?

_____

_____

_____

Chapter 8:

Being The First

Being the first to earn a college degree. The first to make over $100,000. The first to build lasting wealth for your family. The first to consistently keep a roof over your head. The first to raise your children not only as their parent, but as a mentor and an example. Each of these milestones takes real courage and strength. It means putting yourself out there, even when others might not understand. It means remaining genuine and unapologetically you.

Being the first in your family to achieve anything you've set your mind to shows grit, focus, and the kind of determination that changes lives. Being the first among your friends, acquaintances, and your peers shows not just strength—but also courage and vulnerability.

These are accomplishments to be proud of, not things to feel guilty about. Standing apart from what's typical in your circle—and accepting that it's okay to be different—matters more than how others view you. It's normal to feel unsure, to hear the voice of doubt warning that new paths might lead to failure. But when you set firm boundaries against the noise of others, you begin to protect your peace. You come to realize it's okay to want more. It's okay not to settle. It's okay to try and fail—that's where the best lessons are found.

The Success Cycle is putting yourself out there, trying something new, then learning what works and what doesn't. Just as well, the name could be interchanged with: The Failure Cycle, both are ok. And, accurate.

What's not okay is dreaming of more, setting goals, and then letting them slip away by rationalizing excuses, slacking off for no logical reason, or letting others steer your direction. This creates a mindset of failure. Each time you give up on yourself, your mind starts to ask, why even try? That kind of doubt only fuels more excuses.

On the other hand, the more you say you are going to do something—and follow through—the more your mind begins to quiet those negative thoughts. That's why writing down your goals, then taking the **first small step** toward them, matters so much, even if it is so minuscule as making your bed in the morning. This keeps you focused and helps you move forward bit by bit, while building a more positive mindset along the way. Every win throughout your day reinforces that can-do mindset.

I'll be real with you—building a positive mindset isn't easy. It's something you have to work at every single day: It starts with doing what you say you're going to do. Negativity comes easy—it's almost second nature. Our minds are seemingly wired to work against us, constantly whispering all the reasons why something won't work, why we shouldn't try, or why we don't have what it takes. It's way too easy to trap ourselves in fear, excuses, and self-doubt.

We also have this strange habit of treating strangers, coworkers, or even ungrateful family members better than we treat ourselves. We're great at giving solid advice to others but often forget to follow it ourselves. We hype others up, yet drag our feet when it's our own turn. It makes no sense. Why are we so forgiving with others but so hard on ourselves?

Learning to put yourself first is a real journey. It comes with setbacks, failures, discipline, and a lot of trial and error. But you have to keep reminding yourself—it is worth it. You are worth it. Your dreams and goals, are worth it.

Here are a few simple mind tricks that may seem silly—but they work:

> Before you go to bed tonight, tell yourself, "After I get up tomorrow morning, I'm going to make the bed." Then, when you wake up, do it.

> If you have a gym membership, tell yourself before you leave the house, "I'm going to the gym today." Then go.

> When you see that sock on the floor, don't walk past it, just pick up the damn sock.

How about,

"Being the First" — to JUST DO IT!

When you catch yourself not following through on something you said you'd do, take note—either mentally or by writing it down—and then do it as soon as you can. For example, if you leave the room without making your bed, tell yourself, "I promised myself I would make the bed," then go back and do it. Even if making the bed or going to the gym is already part of your routine, get into the habit of saying it, then doing it. Start paying attention to your actions, your conversations, and your daily habits.

Drop the procrastination mindset and replace it with the habit of doing. These small shifts will train your brain to follow through on what you say—without excuses. You're building the habit of trusting yourself by keeping your promises.

Think of it this way: if your boss, your spouse, your parent, or even your sweet old neighbor asks you to do something—you do it. Why? Because not following through might make you seem lazy, lead to guilt, or bring unwanted consequences. And the truth is, you're not lazy.

The point is, if you can show up for others when they ask, then you owe it to yourself to do the same. Be the first to treat yourself with respect, integrity, and honor.

Be bold. Be brave.

Be proud of becoming the first.

You never regret trying.
Pass or fail—you know the answer.
It is in the unknown in which we
have regrets.

On the next page, let's chat about your first...

Being the First: Goals/To do

What have you already done to be the first?

_____

_____

_____

_____

_____

What would you like to be the first at doing?

_____

_____

_____

_____

_____

Accomplishments and Goals:

_____

_____

_____

_____

_____

_____

Section Two

Recapitulation

When it comes to where you are in life and where you want to be, the road can feel tough. Not necessarily in a blood, sweat, and tears kind of way—but in ways that leave you feeling lonely, insecure, or even guilty.

Learning to catch negative thoughts and **Excuses** before they take over—than shifting them back to the truth that you already have what it takes to succeed—is a constant practice in self-awareness.

Chasing your goals, especially when your **Environment** feels like it's working against you, takes strength, discipline, and the ability to think for yourself.

Letting go of certain people in your life starts with recognizing who's truly in your corner and who isn't—That kind of clarity commences by listening closely to the words people use when they speak then taking those words at face-value.

Recognizing the difference between genuine encouragement and unintentional sabotage can be a real eye-opener. When you start listening to your inner voice, the process of letting people go who no longer serve you might be tough—but in the long run, it's one of the best things you can do for yourself.

Switching up your social media by **Keeping It on The Surface** and using it for learning or inspiration can help create a more balanced and relatable profile. It gives people a glimpse of who you are with revealing little personal information. Think of it as a surface-level sneak peek into your soul.

Being The First to take a step forward can feel scary because it requires vulnerability. You're putting yourself out there, unsure whether you'll fail or succeed. But over time, you'll see that every time you take a chance on yourself, you grow. Even the "failures" push you forward by teaching lessons you couldn't learn any other way.

"Faith is unseen but felt, Faith is strength when we feel we have none, Faith is hope when all seems lost."

-   **Catherine Pulsifer**

In the Elimination Phase Section: Environment, People Eliminating, Keeping It on The Surface, and Becoming the First. These are taking a deeper dive into your social life and those closest to you.

In the next section, The Implementation Phase: The new you begins to emerge.

Additional Notes:

SECTION 3

Implementation
Phase

Chapter 9:

Building Your Financial Foundation

I f you receive any amount of money on a consistent basis, you can save. Period. Whether it's one dollar or fifty dollars a week, the amount doesn't matter. The goal is to put money aside without touching it—and learn to pay you before you pay anyone else, including any of your creditors.

What amount of money can you comfortably save each time you get paid? _____

No excuses—just write down the first amount that comes to mind. Is it $5? $25? Maybe $50? Whatever the amount, make sure it's something you can consistently set aside in one of two ways—cash in an envelope stored safely at home, or by transferring it to a savings account linked to your checking account. The preferred method for those who never saved before, don't know where to start, or feel they have "legitimate" reasons—at least in their own mind—for why saving money isn't possible, initially is cash in a drawer. The reason, you can physically see your money stack accumulating—it's a good motivator and test to be sure you can actually leave it alone.

Commitment to yourself:

I will set aside $_____ each week to start saving and growing my money.

If you're already in the habit of saving, your first goal should be to build up your personal checking account. Aim to set aside an amount equal to your total monthly expenses—plus an extra $500.

Here is how to figure that out:

Add up your monthly expenses:

Total bills: $ _____

Total extra expenses: $ _____

Total spending money: $ _____

Any extra costs you think of: $ _____

Let's say your total comes to $3,000. To give yourself some breathing room, aim to build your checking account up to $3,500. This way, you're not living paycheck to paycheck—you'll have saved the equivalent of your monthly expenses, plus a little extra as a cushion.

What is your total monthly spending, plus the $500 extra?

_____

_____

Once you've reached your goal of covering your monthly spending plus a cushion, the next step is to save three months' worth of expenses in your personal savings account—the one linked to your everyday checking. This serves as your safety net in case of an emergency, an unexpected job loss, or simply to give you quick access to funds when needed. With just a few taps on your mobile app, you can move money from savings to checking instantly.

Total monthly spending x 3?

_____

_____

To recap the concept of saving: The money in your checking account helps you avoid living paycheck to paycheck, while the money in your savings account is meant for emergencies and unexpected expenses.

The bigger goal is to let your savings grow and stay untouched—even if you're only saving one dollar at a time.

When you've built the habit of saving instead of spending, and both your checking and savings accounts are in a healthy place, or let's say you're already good at saving and your accounts are already built up, it's time to move on to the next phase—this is where things get exciting. It's time to start making your money work for you.

You'll continue saving as you have been, but with one change: where you're putting your money. Instead of adding more to your standard savings account, add it to a High Yield Money Market Account: It works like a savings account— but with a major boost. While a standard savings account might offer around 0.3% interest, a high yield account typically offers rates above 4%.

There are a few caveats to keep in mind: these accounts require a minimum initial deposit of around $1,000, and you'll need to apply for one. A quick online search can help you find accounts offering the highest interest rates. Some are through local banks, while others are offered by online-only institutions. It depends on what feels right for you.

High Yield Money Market Account:

Local _____ Online Only _____

Start-up: $_____ Interest Rate: _____

The reason I'm introducing the money market account at this stage—rather than as your starting point—is because, despite the name, "Money Market Checking Account," it is actually meant to function like a savings account that you only touch in extreme emergencies. For example, if you need a new refrigerator, you'd use funds from your savings account—the one connected to your everyday checking—leaving the money market account untouched.

The goal is to leave this money alone so it can earn interest, then have that interest earn more interest. It's a safe way for your money to make more money without you doing anything other than continuing to add to it. If saving is still a struggle for you, be cautious—all money market accounts require a minimum balance, dropping below that amount will lead to fees eating up the money you earned from interest.

Once your everyday checking and savings accounts are in a good place, you can link your checking to the money market account and schedule automatic monthly transfers. It might sound complicated, but don't overthink it. Your checking account is solid. Your savings account is in a good place. You're still getting a paycheck—which means you're going to keep saving even MORE. Once you've built up your high-yield money market account to your personal goal, it's time to take the next step.

For the SUPER advanced folks: Let's say you've built up your High Yield Money Market Account to $5,000 and you're now ready to start stepping outside your comfort zone. This is where you choose the slightly riskier type of investment path you want to take next. The possibilities are wide open—but remember:

Higher rewards mean Higher risk.

Choose your comfort level, then start with one option to begin building your portfolio:

- ✓ Stocks/bonds
- ✓ Real Estate
- ✓ Roth IRA
- ✓ Certificate of Deposits (CDs)

Next, decide whether you want to invest on your own or work with a professional. If you're unsure where to start, feel intimidated, or worry about losing your hard-earned money, it might be worth talking to a financial advisor—or at least reading up on your options—so you can make a more informed decision.

Learning about stocks, bonds, or real estate can feel overwhelming. That confusion might cause you to lose interest—or worse, make a poor investment and lose money. Sure, you could take a chance and throw your money into a random stock. Or, you could hire a financial advisor to manage your investments while you take the time to learn how to invest wisely on your own.

Note: A financial advisor is someone who works for you. Their job is to invest your money in a way that fits your current financial situation. Handing over responsibility to someone with experience and training in investing—at least until you feel confident enough to do it yourself—is a smart way to ease into investing with less risk.

That said, here's the caveat: People are people—be cautious when choosing a financial advisor. Some people will say exactly what they think you want to hear just to earn your business. It's up to you to figure out whether their advice is truly in your best interest—or just theirs. There are books out there that can teach you how to choose and interview a financial advisor so you can hold your own during the conversation: Being able to have an "intelligent conversation" means—knowing enough to ask critical questions than having a good understanding those answers.

One of my favorite books on financial advising and money is **MONEY: Mastering the Game by Tony Robbins**. If something more classic is preferred, The Intelligent Investor by Benjamin Graham is jam packed with valuable insight on investing—fair warning, it's a long read.

Whether you choose to play it safe by starting your investment journey with an I-bond or CD (Certificate of Deposit), or decide to take a bolder step by reaching out to a financial advisor—you're making progress, and that's something to be proud of.

**Start off slow,
Learn to watch your money grow.**

Recap:

First Step toward Financial Freedom

Saving in checking > Saving in standard savings > Saving in High Yield Money Market account > Saving through Investing in: Stocks, bonds, real estate, etcetera.

Recap:

Initial ideal amount in each of the following, in this order.

Checking: Total monthly expenses + $500
Standard Savings: Three months' worth of total expenses
High-Yield Money Market: $5,000
All other monies: Invest

Note: Once you have learned all the basics, you can change the amounts and investment options as you see fit. Some people chose to keep minimal amounts in their standard accounts opting to throw all monies into riskier investment options or retirement accounts. It's all personal prefer-ence. These are guidelines to get you started.

Building Your Money: Goals

Personal Checking Goal: $ _____

Connected Savings Goal: $ _____

High Yield Money Market Goal: $ _____

What is your first step to accomplishing these goals:

_____

_____

What extra expenses can you eliminate to save more?

_____

_____

_____

What is your next book to read on saving your money and investing your money?

_____

_____

_____

_____

_____

Chapter 10:

Accountability

L et's call accountability for what it is: **owning your shit!** For some, it's a gradual process of taking ownership of your mindset, your actions, and how you react. For others, the lightbulb goes off immediately: they admit it and make the changes right then and there. How you respond to situations throughout the day usually depends on your mindset in that moment. Some people need serious work in the accountability department. Others—Maybe a few adjustments.

The bottom line is, we all need to hold ourselves to a higher standard when it comes to accountability. Here's a reality check: When you react, you're showing yourself that your mind is so weak someone else's actions have the power to control yours. It's wild when you really think about it, you're a strong, goal-driven, independent thinker who wants to stand out—yet, you are letting someone else's nonsense dictate your behavior?

Take driving, for example. When another driver tailgates you, cuts you off, or is clearly texting in the left lane, how do you respond:

- o Do you calmly go around them?
- o Do you move over and let them pass?
- o Do you start yelling, flashing hand gestures, and getting petty right back?

More importantly, do you let these moments affect you for a while afterward? If so, why?

_____

_____

In any situation, sometimes it is more peaceful for you if you simply look at that person and say...

"They Don't Know No Better"

Look at their facial expression—can you see the cluelessness? The ignorance? The obliviousness? Most of the time, you can. In those moments, shift your mindset to: They don't know no better. Let out a little chuckle, then move on.

Finding short sayings that help lighten your mood can go a long way in changing how you respond to situations. We can't always control the circumstances around us, but we can control how we react to them. Even with family—or especially with kids—it's important to learn how to pick your battles.

Ask yourself:

o Who's really going to "win" this?
o Is this worth the energy or the argument?

Only you can decide what's truly worth the effort. Sometimes it's better to make your point; other times, it's best to just let it go. Majority of the time, it's small stuff in the grand scheme of things. Taking a second to consider the ramifications—or knowing the overall context— helps you make better choices in the heat of a conversation.

Perhaps asking yourself:

- o Is this my bridge to cross—or burn?
- o Should this be discussed in private?
- o Is this conversation directly related to me?
- o If I share my opinion, will the other person actually hear it—or are they too set in their ways?

Flipping the script—are you taking accountability for your actions during conversations that turned confrontational?

Could you have:

- o Listened more?
- o Spoken in a different tone?
- o Misunderstood their words?
- o Taken a pause prior to responding?

- o Created expectations in your head based on how you thought the other person should respond?
- o Asked questions that take a more in-depth look into the conversation,
  - "How did that make you feel?"
  - "Would you like my opinion?"
  - "What do you need from me?"

All our minds work differently, and the way we interpret situations can vary just as much. Two people could be in the same place, at the same time, looking at the same thing—yet one sees a red shirt, and the other sees pink.

Emotions work in the same way, what feels like heartbreak to you might feel like freedom to someone else. What looks like a red flag to you might show up as pink to someone else. Maybe they'll dip a toe in to see how it plays out, while you've already turned around and ran the in the other direction.

Interpretation is personal—it's shaped by layers of your own past experiences. It's the story you are telling yourself and not what the other person may actual be saying. Owning and understanding this is a form of accountability and growth—recognizing that your view of a situation or conversation is just that—your view.

As you go through your day replay your actions. Keep a journal. Reflect often. I like to play some soft music, sip on a glass of wine then reflect on my day: giving way to changes and gratitude. The more you analyze your responses to situations and what people are truly saying during those interactions, the faster you'll start building a stronger mindset; Eventually taking words at face value becomes instinctual.

Accountability Goal/To do

Write down a few sayings that you can use to change your mindset?

_____

_____

_____

In what areas can you take accountability?

_____

_____

_____

_____

_____

I can improve my reaction to situations by,

_____

_____

_____

_____

_____

_____

_____

Chapter 11:

On The Daily

Every day, you owe it to yourself to raise your quality of life and be your own cheerleader. You've got a good head on your shoulders—when you make a decision, it means you've thought through the possibilities and have chosen what works best for you.

Some decisions come in a flash. Others take time to process. Either way—be proud of it. Own it. Even when it's hard. Even when it hurts someone's feelings. Even if it turns out to be the wrong call. If you made that decision with integrity and good intentions, then it was the right one for you in that moment.

The right decision isn't always the easy decision.

Your new goal is to decide—each morning when you wake up:

Today, I am going to...

Read a Chapter: Pick a book that benefits you. It could be the Bible, a book about cars, or anything that aligns with your goals, interests, or personal growth. Reading just one chapter—whether before bed, on your lunch break, or while sipping coffee—can help you build a positive habit of learning and open your mind to new ideas.

> ➤ **For men:** "Man's Search for Meaning" by Viktor Frankl offers powerful insights in your darkest moments.
> ➤ **For everyone:** "The Alchemist" by Paulo Coelho is a motivational story on trusting your intuition and chasing your dreams.

View Your Vision Board: Create a vision board or use a whiteboard with a removable sticker-back, hang it in your bedroom. Update it often to reflect your aspirations and evolving goals.

Create a Task List: Before bed, jot down a short list of things to do the next day. This clears your mind, helps you sleep better, and mentally prepares you for the day ahead.

Celebrate Small Wins: Finishing little tasks each day builds momentum. Whether it's making your bed, going to the gym, completing a project, or keeping a negative comment to yourself—every effort matters. Acknowledge it.

Do It Now: Follow Through Immediately. If something comes to mind, act on it before you leave the room. Procrastination builds subconscious stress. Every time you pass the car that needs washing or laundry that needs folding, it lingers in the back of your mind.

Building the habit of handling tasks as they come helps reduce stress: lowering cortisol levels.

Listen to Inspiration: YouTube, podcasts, or audiobooks are great tools for your mental health. They motivate, boost confidence, and help shift your mindset toward positivity.

Start replacing passive background noise during your commute or workout with encouraging and uplifting content.

Be Proud: Give yourself grace and show some appreciation by celebrating your wins throughout the day. Showing gratitude and appreciation boosts positivity and supports your well-being.

Pause, smile, and acknowledge your effort—big or small appreciate it all. You're doing wonderful !

Do Hard Things: Every day, push yourself to do something that feels challenging—whatever "hard" means to you. If it feels uncomfortable, even better. It doesn't have to be a big thing. Maybe it's skipping going out for a beer to read a book, saying no to junk food, trying a new machine at the gym, or applying for a job you don't think you're qualified for.

"The difference between try and triumph is a little 'umph'."

- **Marvin Phillips**

Growth comes from stepping outside your comfort zone then deciding to live, think and act slightly better than the day before—the epitome of stepping outside your norm: it's deciding every day to reflect on your behavior and outcomes then challenging yourself to make provisions for the upcoming day. I encourage you, On The Daily, to raise the quality of your life and the lives of those surrounding you.

Be Brave. Be Spontaneous. Be Audacious.

On The Daily: Goals/To Do

What will it take to become the best version of you?

_____

_____

_____

_____

Today I am going to:

Read a Chapter: _____

Revise My Vision board: _____

Create My Task List: _____

Celebrate Small Wins: _____

Do It Now: _____

Listen to Inspiration: _____

Be Proud of: _____

Do One Hard Thing: _____

Additional Notes:

_____

_____

_____

_____

Chapter 12:

First Step

I N previous chapters we chatted about how the excuses we conjure up are fears from our subconscious doubts aiming to protect us from, what we are telling ourselves is, failure. Some of these fears stem from the environment we come from or are currently in. While others, stem from conversations with the ones closest to us who come across as solid intentions, but are fueled by unknowingly projecting their own fears, from their past experiences and trauma, onto us. We then discussed empowering ways to rebuttal excuses thereby clearing our minds from the extra negative chatter—owning our shit, moving in silence, and intently listening to the words people are saying when conversating are a few ways to combat an accumulation of un-healthy thoughts, allowing us to embrace more forward-thinking thoughts. Throughout all of this we have taken many First Steps by taking a deeper dive into what we envision our lives to be, then taking actionable steps—making the tough decisions to remove people, including our family, from our social media pages and personal lives, committing to investing in ourselves, and through putting the effort in to raise the quality of our lives, and those around us.

Setting goals—no matter the size—should always be our top priority. When thinking in terms of how we live our lives, everything we do is, in fact, setting a goal then figuring out how to make that goal come to fruition. We figure out what it is that we want then break it down into manageable steps until we reach achievement. This literally pertains to every move we make in life: Getting a job, relationships, raising children, and in every way that we live our lives—we decide what we want then figure out how to get it. If we can't initial get it, then we make the decision to take a new path or dig a little deeper to find a work-around. Any way you want to spin it, the bottom line, what we want is the goal and how we get what we want, are the actionable steps we take to achieve said goal; therefore, we are intentionally or unintentionally always setting goals. And as we have discovered, the more intentional we are—the more control we have over the outcome.

Taking control of our outcomes, and life, as a whole, is the sole purpose of my writings. The goal is to live each day purposefully—with intent.

- ✓ Intentionally creating a positively-driven mindset regarding your financials.
- ✓ Intentionally surrounding ourselves with remarkably kind, genuinely-loving people.
- ✓ Intentionally, and selfishly, making the best decisions for you.

Creating a plan for achieving all your dreams and goals by learning, then embracing the profound concept of: **One Step, The First Step** is the last part of our journey. This concept is simple and boils down to figuring out the very first actionable step you need to move forward with achieving your goal while acknowledging everything else is irrelevant. Thinking too far ahead only clutters your mind, creates unnecessary stress, and could possibly set you up for actual failure—not lesson-based failure. Like, never amounting to anything failure.

Every goal is written the same way: with only **O**ne **S**tep—**THE FIRST STEP**.

Examples of two goals:

Goal 1: Take Community College course.
First Step: Make appointment with a Student Advisor.

That's it. That's your start. Once you've made the appointment, erase then replace. **Your new First Step becomes:** Go to the appointment.

That conversation will guide you towards the next steps, like applying for financial aid, setting up the initial testing appointment, or registering for classes.

Recap the Simplicity: Use a whiteboard in your bedroom.
Write down your goal:
"Take a class at the Community College."
Write down your current first step:
"Make an appointment w/ a student advisor."

As your goal progresses apply the: Erase then Replace method.
<u>Erase:</u> Make appointment with an advisor
<u>Replace:</u> Go to the appointment add Date/time

As you can see, by only writing down your next step, you avoid feeling overwhelmed, fabricating excuses, and it takes all the "what ifs" out of the equation making you to cross that bridge when, or if, that time comes.

Let's look at another hypothetical goal, one of my personal favorites: Becoming a motorcycle rider.

Goal 2: Becoming a Motorcycle Rider
First Step: Go to a motorcycle dealership

Browsing images online won't cut it. Go to the dealership, sit on bikes—feeling the excitement (or nerves). I am sure a salesperson will approach you, that conversation will guide you on what your next first step is. Otherwise, you're gonna fill your head with all the typical excuses:

- I don't have good credit.
- I don't know if I can afford it.
- I don't have my license.
- I still have to take a riding course.

Blah, blah, blah. You're stressing about a license and affordability for something you're not even sure you're ready to ride. These examples of excuses are examples of the stories you create in your head—the mental clutter. Pro tip: You don't need a license to buy a motorcycle. And why spend money on a license if you don't even own a bike? I know so many people that have a license then don't get a bike until years later, if at all. See how all these so-called "requirements" are really just distraction also known as—Excuses.

Recap the Simplicity: On whiteboard,
Write down your goal:
Becoming a Motorcycle Rider
Write down your current first step:
Go to the dealership.

As your goal progresses,
Erase: Go to the dealership
Replace: with your NEW first step.

This method works with every goal, of every size, for everything you want to accomplish in life. Begin by reviewing your goals you wrote down in the chapter on Setting Goals. Focus on one step at a time to keep your goals comprehensible—Stay motivated and build momentum.

MOST IMPORTANTLY: Do not talk about your goals with anyone. It'll only invite doubt. You want it? Do it. That simple. Wipe out the noise, set the goal, then decide on the very first step: Everything else will fall into place.

The Power of the First Step:

I don't care what your circumstances are, who you are, or what excuses your mind keeps throwing at you—**stop overthinking.**

Focus on the first step, and you will find a way forward. Everything will fall into place as it is supposed to.

You cannot predict how an event will play out, but we can **predict your next move**. Period.

"One part at a time, one day at a time, we can accomplish any goal we set for ourselves."

                    - **Karen Casey**

First Step: Goals/To do

Going back to page 25, write 2 Goals:

Median: _____

First Step: _____

Grand: _____

First Step: _____

Is there any reason you cannot take The First Step on the next business day?

_____

_____

If so, then this is not the actual first step. How can you break it down further?

_____

_____

Additional Notes:

_____

_____

_____

_____

Section Three

Recapitulation

T aking control of your future through actionable steps is the ultimate form of self-love. It means going after what you want— and what you're destined for—with credence. It's you showing up for you, refusing to let excuses or skepticism get in your way.

Taking responsibility for your decisions and maintaining **Accountability** for those decisions will, over time, build a strong sense of assertiveness. You begin to take ownership of your actions, mindset, and reactions with poise—no matter what challenges come your way.

Building Your Financial Foundation is a powerful contribution toward investing in yourself. It takes strength and discipline to watch your money grow through consistency and intentional saving. Acknowledge your progress: be grateful for your ability to set money aside.

Achieving small wins each day originates with building habits—**On The Daily.** It's a gradual process of persistence, positive reinforcement, repetition, and taking on hard tasks. It's a matter of developing a routine that encourages growth, learning, and new ways of thinking.

In the chapter: **First Step,** we talked about how breaking down goals into **one** manageable endeavor helps reduce the stress and anxiety that often come when a goal seems to have a gazillion steps prior to coming to fruition. Simplifying the process into one clear action—The First Step—eradicates excuses and makes forward movement predictable.

"The moment you doubt whether you can fly, you cease forever to be able to do it."

- J.M. Barrie

Be cognizant:

"The only limit to the height of your achievements is the reach of your dreams and your willingness to work for them."

- Michelle Obama

"It's not enough to take steps which may someday lead to a goal, each step must be itself a goal and a step likewise."

-   **Johann Wolfgang Von Goethe**

First Steps in a Nutshell

Chapter One—No Excuses

FIRST Step: Acknowledge they are all excuses.

Chapter Two—Reading to Learn

FIRST Step: Buy a book.

Chapter Three—Setting Goals

FIRST Step: Make a goal.

Chapter Four—Money In, Money Out

FIRST Step: Write down monthly expenses.

Chapter Five—Environment Mean Nothing

FIRST Step: Change your perspective.

Chapter Six—Eliminating People

FIRST Step: Listen intently to people

Chapter Seven—Keep it on the Surface

FIRST Step: Move in silence

Chapter Eight—Being the First

FIRST Step: Correlate courage with vulnerability

Chapter Nine—

Building Your Financial Foundation

FIRST Step: Discipline your spending

Chapter Ten—Accountability

FIRST Step: Own your shit

Chapter Eleven—On The Daily

FIRST Step: Invest in you

Chapter Twelve—First Step

FIRST Step: Get a wall sticker whiteboard

The Inside Scoop

E ver since I was a little girl, I knew I was different. I never had a clear dream or profession that called to me—I just knew I was meant for more than what the people around me seemed to expect for themselves. I've always felt poles apart from those surrounding me, if that makes sense. When it came to setting goals, mine was simple: make it through the day without getting into trouble.

Even as a young kid, my version of daydreaming was figuring out how to make money on my own—without needing anyone else. I'd spend my days searching under vending machines for coins, braiding colorful strings into people's hair, making friendship bracelets, and turning a patch of grass into my very own candy shop.

By early teens, I landed an unofficial job after school. I'd get dropped off in random neighborhoods, going door-to-door selling $5 items out of a milk crate for a guy who picked us up in an old over-sized work van. He never met our parents, never shared any business info, and only hired kids.

Looking back, it was definitely sketchy—but it worked for me. We'd be dropped off around 4 p.m. then picked up around 9. At the end of the day, I walked away with cash in hand. Whether I showed up the next day was completely up to me—but of course, I was there every single day.

I got good at making up sympathetic stories to sell my items, and soon, I started challenging myself to sell out my entire milk crate by the end of the night. It became a game—a competition with myself. How much money could I make in the time I had? That little hustle gave me a sense of independence and financial freedom.

Even at 12 years old, I was creating a world of my own. By the time I was 15, I finally had the chance to leave and be on my own. My love for earning money and having freedom only grew— because now I had total independence. The downside? I was truly alone. And the trauma I carried became a dangerous mix with freedom, stirring up deep self-doubt that worked against me. I told myself: Whenever something good happens, something bad is sure to follow.

I carried that belief like a chip on my shoulder, constantly questioning: What's the point of trying when I'll just mess it up, or something else will as soon as I start getting somewhere? To me, relying on others— showing vulnerability—meant I was weak. It meant I wasn't strong enough to make it on my own.

Looking back now, I realize how much of that was self-sabotage. When people say, we are our own worst enemy, they're talking about that exact thing. We talk ourselves out of opportunities, box ourselves in, and convince ourselves we're not good enough. We create excuses. We put limits on ourselves.

After years of mental ups and downs, I finally started listening to motivational speakers—Jim Rohn, Les Brown, Tony Robbins, Steve Harvey, Eric Thomas—people I now think of as mentors, (even if only in my mind.) I believe the male, dominant characters resonated with me since I related more with my masculine half.

In my darkest moments, hearing their words, I held onto the belief that I was meant for more. My mindset shifted from Why me? to Why not me?

Why couldn't I be the first in my family to build generational wealth? Why couldn't I make a lot of money? If they can rise from nothing to succeed, then so can I. I learned to keep the endgame in mind from the very beginning. Whatever your goals, break them down to only the first step to get the ball rolling.

Each step becoming your new First Step.

Challenge yourself: How daring can you be? How bold can you be? How brave can you be?

I believe you're capable of being more daring, bolder, and braver than you even realize.

"Set your goals so high that striving for them transforms who you are in the process."

- unknown

My final words of wisdom to you...

Always stay faithful and on guard,
it is in the moments of change
the enemy perceives weakness.
It is these moments we are our strongest.

With Lots of Love,
From me, your newest cheerleader,
♡ Stephanie ♡

A Special Thank You

To my mother: You taught me how I want to be in life by showing me how not to be. I also learned how to raise my girls by understanding what not to do. For that, I am truly grateful.

To my friends: The ones who turned out not to be the kind of friend, to me that I was to them: lessons were learned. Every experience helped me grow. Thank you for that.

To all my adopted mothers: The women who took me under their wings and showed me I was valued, worthy, and that my life had meaning: I appreciate you more than words can express. Thank you for keeping me on track.

To my Hooli Hoooo: You know who you are. Through every high and low, you have been my steady, unconditional support person—I can tell you anything without fear of judgment. I admire your unspoken strength and your kind heart tucked beneath that ruthless exterior. I truly adore you.

To My lovely Girls:

Felicity and Serenity,

I never realized how much I needed you both to pull me through the "hard" part of life and keep me grounded. You are my driving forces, pushing me to grow and accomplish more than I ever thought possible. I dedicate everything I am to both of you. I will always be your biggest fan.

To the person this book makes a difference for: I hope you keep going. I believe in you.

To everyone who helped bring this book to life:
Lucy S (Fiverr) – Editor extraordinaire. @lucy_format
Aimee Calderon (Fiverr) – Assisted Editor
Yasir Nadeem (Fiverr) – Cover art & Design

Jennifer Shore – You inspired me to write for a broader audience; without that conversation, this book wouldn't exist. Thank you! Special shoutout to Curt.

Thank you for all who had a hand in

making this book come to life!

Disclaimer: No affiliations to the books or music mentioned.

<u>Secret Chapter:</u>
For Men Only

For most of my life, my masculine side tended to overpower my feminine side. Growing up on my own at a young age—without real parental guidance—and living in unpleasant neighborhoods turned me into, at times, a little wild monster. My tough exterior made me feel like I didn't need anyone, and I carried that chip on my shoulder for years. I still remember my first physical fight; I was around eight. My best friend and I were outside arguing when, out of nowhere, a circle formed around us. Someone shoved me into her, and just like that, the fight started. In that moment, my best friend became my enemy, and there was no way I was going to let anyone get the best of me. Even as a little kid, I felt like I had something to prove.

That chip only got bigger as I got older. Well into adulthood, I believed "talking it out" was weak, and yelling meant someone had gotten under my skin. To avoid that, I'd swing first instead of using my words. Looking back now, I see there was anger, misplaced pride, and what I thought was strength—was actually my biggest weakness. It's easy to swing first. It's easy to hide behind toughness. It's easy to blame others instead of taking a hard look at ourselves and owning our part.

I used to believe that showing feelings—crying, asking for help, or admitting I needed someone: being vulnerable in any way—was signs of failure. I convinced myself that if I couldn't fix my own problems, nobody else could. Talking about what was going on in my life felt pointless because I didn't think anyone really cared. Besides, I was going to do what I wanted anyway, so why bother with anyone else's opinion, I wouldn't listen.

There was a time when, no matter what happened, I would just acknowledge it, shrug, and move on. In my mind, there was no point in "dealing" with anything. People close to me often said I was cold-hearted—that I didn't care about anyone or anything but myself. But the truth is, none of that was real. I've always had an incredibly giving heart. Fighting never made me happy; it just kept me up for hours afterward, replaying everything in my head, thinking about how I should've—or could've—handled it differently.

Usually, those thoughts involved more violent scenarios that could've landed me in captivity. (That's my polite way of saying jail.)

Looking back, I have realized:

It is not: That I didn't want opinions—I just didn't respect anyone in my circle enough to listen to what they had to say.

It is not: That I had a hard exterior—I simply learned to defend myself the only way I knew how.

It is not: That I was unemotional—I just had to stay strong to survive and provide for myself.

It is not: That I didn't need anyone—It's that the one time I did ask for help, I was met with false promises and no real follow-through. So, I taught myself to manage alone.

It is not: That I couldn't be "fixed"—I just didn't know who I was or what I truly wanted out of life because I was too busy living in the moment, trying to survive.

It is not: That I didn't care about the hardships happening to me or around me—I had just been through so much that I felt numb. That was my coping mechanism.

Now, I'm not saying I can fully relate to you—a man. I'm very much so a woman, and I'll never truly know what it feels like to walk in your shoes. But what I have noticed is so many men, especially younger ones, often think and feel the same way. They avoid emotions, handle problems with violence, run from the pain, or lean on distractions like sports, drugs, alcohol, or "good times," a.k.a. random females, instead of dealing with what's really going on inside.

For those of you, with that mindset, **I have a few words of wisdom:**

- ❖ **Vulnerability is strength.** Walking away, is strength. Limiting your circle to people you respect, is strength. Putting yourself first, is strength. Releasing yourself from the pressure of carrying the world's problems—that, too, is strength.
- ❖ **Carrying the Weight.** You don't have to carry everything on your shoulders. Other people's burdens are not yours to bear. Setting boundaries—with yourself and with others—is strength.

Discovering who you really are and learning to carry yourself in alignment with that truth takes both strength and vulnerability. But once you do, it allows you to serve yourself first—and in turn, serve your partner and loved ones in a healthier, more meaningful way. When you unapologetically own who you are and what you want, you'll experience deeper connections, more fulfilling moments, and greater success in life.

❖ **Be kind to yourself and others.** Learn to be intentional and selective with your time and energy. Don't hand out yeses out of guilt or habit. Work harder on yourself than you do for anyone else—including your employer or even your family.

❖ **Listen to Strong Men Speak.** Take time to listen to a strong man speak—someone whose lessons come from real life, from their pain and growth, and from failures and successes.'

Their words can help you uncover the strength already inside you—guiding you to become the best version of yourself.

Some of my favorite strong male speakers—men I love listening to and highly recommend—are

Eric Thomas, Les Brown, Tony Robbins, Trent Shelton, Jim Rohn and Steve Harvey. They've each written multiple books and have countless motivational videos available online.

Start there, and let their experience and wisdom push you forward.

Showing up for yourself will allow you to show up for others.

P.S. Woman are reading, **"Act Like A Lady, Think Like A Man"** By Steve Harvey. This is a game changer; woman are going to revert to the day when men had to step up. So, GET YOUR SHIT Together!

Dax - "To Be A Man"
    Jelly Roll - "Unpretty"
        ...These songs...Powerful

For Men Only: Goals/To Do

Do you carry extra weight on your shoulders? Why.

_____

_____

Do you use females or other vices as an escape?

_____

_____

Do you feel you need to be where you want to be in life before you fully commit yourself to another?

_____

If so, what's 1 or 2 goal(s) you would like to reach?

_____

_____

_____

As a man, yes, you are the predominate provider; however, you should also have a partner that has your back when needed. Do you feel you have that (if you currently have a partner)?

_____

_____

_____

Additional Notes:

QR Code to purchase
Change A Smile, Change A Life

Open phone camera > hold camera up to image > a
link will appear on phone screen (Ingramspark)

($25.00 plus S & H)

A book for those in the
Dental Industry

If you love your dentist, grab a copy of this book

for them.

They will thank you.

A portion of the proceeds goes toward

dental care packages for low-income

communities and Women & Children Centers.

Available May 2025

Clean A Smile, Change YOUR Life

AuthorStephanieWelker@Gmail.com

for details

A book for the Dental Hygienist in your life.

If you love your teeth cleaner person, grab a copy
of this book for them.
They will thank you.

A portion of the proceeds goes toward
dental care packages for low-income
communities and Women & Children Centers.

For: Speaking Events, Success Stories, Thoughts & Coaching

AuthorStephanieWelker@Gmail.com